

UNIVERSITY CASEBOOK SERIES

EDITORIAL BOARD

ROBERT C. CLARK

DIRECTING EDITOR

Dean & Royall Professor of Law
Harvard University

DANIEL A. FARBER

Henry J. Fletcher Professor of Law University of Minnesota

OWEN M. FISS

Sterling Professor of Law Yale University

GERALD GUNTHER

William Nelson Cromwell Professor of Law, Emeritus Stanford University

THOMAS H. JACKSON

President University of Rochester

HERMA HILL KAY

Dean & Barbara Nachtrieb Armstrong Professor of Law University of California, Berkeley

HAROLD HONGJU KOH

Gerard C. & Bernice Latrobe Smith Professor of International Law Yale Law School

DAVID W. LEEBRON

Dean & Lucy G. Moses Professor of Law Columbia University

SAUL LEVMORE

William B. Graham Professor of Law University of Chicago

ROBERT L. RABIN

A. Calder Mackay Professor of Law Stanford University

CAROL M. ROSE

Gordon Bradford Tweedy Professor of Law & Organization Yale University

DAVID L. SHAPIRO

William Nelson Cromwell Professor of Law Harvard University